Closer
To The
Father

21 Day Prayer Devotional

Meet Josh online and receive additional study
materials at **JoshPaul.org**

Join Josh on a mission trip in the Appalachian Mountains!
Visit **AnchorRidge.org** to learn more.

Come to a live taping of Josh's TV show! Register at **AnchorRidge.org**

Contents

Introduction

I will never forget the impact that my first 21-day prayer and fast had on my life. It was an unforgettable event! In this regard, I have been sharing it with people for the last 10 years for testimonial purposes and so that others can be motivated and be hopeful.

At that time, I read about a study that had been done which claimed that humans can learn new behaviors and enforce new, positive habits in just 21 days. Think of it as a 'reset' period if you will.

Having tested the water and proved them to be deep, I encourage you to get out your calendar and block off the next 21 days. Commit on a level that says, 'I refuse to give up, I'm going all-in on this!' However, I have to warn you in advance; the first 3 days will most likely prove to be the most difficult as your body is trying to adjust to "dying to self,"… but after all, that is what God's Word calls us to do.

At the end of 21 days, my hope is that you will have a more intimate relationship with God - one that ignites the Fruit of the Spirit in your everyday life. Certainly, when we add fasting to prayer, it increases our awareness of God and helps us focus on Him, to better see Him and ourselves in a brighter light, bringing positive changes.

Get real; be completely open and honest with yourself and God in the 'notes' section of each day's prayer. Moreover, for it to be more effective, we need to get past ourselves, our pride, and our own will so we can hear what God is asking us to do, to let go of, or even step in to. The fact that you picked up this book says you want more, but you must ask yourself… How badly do I want it? Is it bad enough to commit for the next 21 days?!?! THINK ABOUT IT…You are just 21 days away from a better prayer life, a closer walk with God, and, with fasting, most likely a healthier body. Go all in!

What if I miss a day? No problem! Get right back to it. We are human, and God gives us grace, just do your very best, whatever that looks like for you. Challenge yourself. Push yourself. You are capable of far more than you think. Winning starts in the mind. If you make up in your mind in the beginning that nothing will get you off track, you have already won the victory. Set your mind and keep it set on things above. Every morning get up and declare a day of victory. Every evening, thank God for battles won as He brings you through this journey.

Of course people get a little nervous when you start talking about fasting, but, I want you to start slow. Don't get nervous! This devotional recommends picking one thing each day. Pick anything you want! Anything from coffee, your favorite soda, gossip, television, meat, or even no food at all. You could go big and say no social media for 8 hours! You'll be surprised in the spiritual difference it makes when you deny yourself to seek God. I also want you to take time each day to write down what you are thankful for. It can be absolutely anything— your dog, tomatoes, air conditioning, anything at all. When we start each day with a grateful heart, it brightens the day and reminds us of God's blessings. Don't forget to pick one person each day to go out and purposely be a blessing to! It makes the day so fun! Turn the page to begin your journey to a better you.

.

Day 1: Draw Near To God

James 4:8 Draw near to God and He will draw near to you. Cleanse *your* hands, *you* sinners; and purify *your* hearts, *you* double-minded.

God, I pray that You would open the eyes of my heart to see You in all things, everywhere I go. My hearts desire is to be close to You and to do Your will. Cleanse me oh Lord and give me a pure heart! Help me to evaluate my life and get rid of things that are keeping me from spending time in Your Word. I desperately need Your Word.

Open the eyes of my spirit so I can see the colors of true love; Love that only comes from Heaven. Help me to let go of anything that is causing strife in my life. My human flesh wants to hold onto past hurts, but I know I need to let go of these things, because they are creating space between You and I. I want to be as close as I can get.

I know I will never be perfect on this side of Heaven, but I want to please You and do Your will. Help me to crucify this flesh, regardless of what is going on around me. There are always reasons and excuses to do things "my way," but I pray You would remind me daily that my life turns out better when I honor You in all things and take your direction. Help me to know when it's Your call.

I know it is not You who has moved if I feel distance between us. Help me to bring all I am to You today, to lay it at Your feet; to be restored in the areas I need restoration. My heart wants to be closer to You. Purify me as I press in to draw near to You. I need Your Help.

In the name of Jesus I pray, amen.

Thought For The Day: My Public display of Christianity is nothing without a powerful, meaningful, prayer life.

Day 1

Notes (Go ahead and mark it up! The key is to be REAL. This is just you and God.)

_____

_____

_____

_____

_____

_____

_____

_____

_____

5 Things I Am Thankful For Today Are:

_____

_____

_____

_____

_____

Today I Will Fast _____ for 8 hours.

Someone I Can Be A Blessing To Today:

_____

Day 2: Teach Me To Seek Your Face

2 Chronicles 7:14 If My people who are called by My name will humble themselves, and pray and seek My face, and turn from their wicked ways, then I will hear from heaven, and will forgive their sin and heal their land.

God, I pray that You would teach me how to seek Your face. I pray that You would help me to turn from anything that is not of You and fill those places in me with the power to live for You. Please show me any sin in my life that I am not aware of; short comings where You would like me to come up higher. Search the depths of my heart and begin to replace old habits and mindsets with your Word.

I want my life to count - I want to be a shining vessel of what it looks like to be entirely transformed by a perfect King. I desperately need Your help laying aside every weight that so easily besets me. I need Your discernment from falling into traps set by the enemy. My life is Yours so I lay down my will at Your feet and give You full control.

I want to do whatever it takes to please You; to live in a way that makes me more aware of You in everyday moments. Help me to let go and forgive myself for the things I did in the past that I can never go back and change. You have forgiven me, so Lord help me forgive myself.

Help me to experience the full power available in the Name of Jesus. Help me to be covered in Your love and Your presence so that when I go out into the world I am dripping with Your goodness. Strengthen me so I can help lift others up and show them Your goodness.

I want nothing in this world more than I want a relationship with You; to finish my race, complete my purpose, and do all You have called me to do. Help me to live for You.

In the name of Jesus I pray, amen.

Thought For The Day: Everywhere I show up today I am carrying the power and presence of God.

Day 2

Notes (Go ahead and mark it up! The key is to be REAL. This is just you and God.)

_____

_____

_____

_____

_____

_____

_____

_____

_____

_____

5 Things I Am Thankful For Today Are:

_____

_____

_____

_____

_____

Today I Will Fast _____ for 8 hours.

Someone I Can Be A Blessing To Today:

_____

Day 3: Grow My Faith To Do All Things

Hebrews 11:6 But without faith *it is* impossible to please *Him,* for he who comes to God must believe that He is, and *that* He is a rewarder of those who diligently seek Him.

Father, I come into Your presence and bow my life to You. All I am is in You and all I have is Yours.

I need your help. For the path I'm called, I will need more faith. Help me to realize that You are with me everywhere I go and that You love me more than I could ever imagine. Help me to GET IT! I hear these truths all the time, but help me to understand and put it to practice in my daily life.

Give me the courage to grow my faith by believing You and I, together, can do all things. I am walking around with the Creator of the universe living on the inside of me! You have already proved that nothing is too big for You. Help me deal with the thoughts in my head that tell me I haven't lived a good enough life for You to move on my behalf; to remember that You don't move in situations based on what I have done, but based on who You are.

According to your Word, God, I want to please You. I want to be fully devoted, bringing you every single piece of me. Even the darkest parts that I am uncomfortable with or that I don't like. You made me and know me completely. Remind me, moment by moment that seeking

You is not a big event, but it is in the everyday living out of Your Word and listening to the still small voice that directs me toward Your will for my life and brings peace to my inner soul.

I believe Jesus died on the cross for me. I believe that I'm saved. I have faith! Help me to put it to work for You in other areas of my life to bring glory to Your Name in the earth. In the name of Jesus I pray, Amen.

Thought For The Day: Faith is the currency of the Kingdom of God. It is the 'title deed' to the thing I am believing God for. I own it in the Spirit before it becomes made manifest in the physical.

Day 3

Notes (Go ahead and mark it up! The key is to be REAL - this is just you and God.)

_____

_____

_____

_____

_____

_____

_____

_____

_____

_____

5 Things I Am Thankful For Today Are:

_____

_____

_____

_____

_____

Today I Will Fast _____ for 8 hours.

Someone I Can Be A Blessing To Today:

_____

Day 4: Not My Will, But Yours Lord

Luke 22:42 ..saying, "Father, if it is Your will, take this cup away from Me; nevertheless not My will, but Yours, be done."

Father, I come to You amid everything going on in my life. I know You hear me and I know You understand the struggles I face. I need Your help to move forward. To reach greater heights.

Strengthen my spirit to do Your will without first asking myself if I like it or what I think about it. When You speak, my answer is yes and amen. When You call, I will come - even if it makes no sense to the human me. Your promises are sure; ALL THINGS are working out for the good of those who love God and are called according to Your purpose, and I trust that. I trust You. Even in the middle of a storm, I will trust You.

I don't want to take the easy road - I want to take whatever path You call me down. Daily, I will pray again and again, not my will, but Thine be done. I trust Your plan for my life and I know You wouldn't ask me to do something that I couldn't do. Im equipped for this. Your Spirit is in me. I am so much stronger than I think I am. I have yet to see what I am capable of and what we can do together as I keep submitting myself to You.

Through all of this, I want to know the depths of your heart. You keep moving me from having the mindset of a servant to a mindset of a child of The King. Continue to open my eyes to the way You see me, to the way You love me. It keeps changing me to know someone like You can love someone like me in such an unstoppable, passionate, never-ending kind of way. Help me to rest in that. Help me to take refuge in Your goodness.

More than anything in this world, I want to know Your heart and to do Your will. Above my own will, above my plans, above anything this world may try to offer me, I choose You. Help me to walk closer to You everyday.

In the name of Jesus, amen.

Thought For The Day: I can and will do whatever it takes. I have the power of God living in me, I can do this.

Day 4

Notes (Go ahead and mark it up! The key is to be REAL. This is just you and God.)

_____

_____

_____

_____

_____

_____

_____

_____

_____

_____

5 Things I Am Thankful For Today Are:

_____

_____

_____

_____

_____

Today I Will Fast _____ for 8 hours.

Someone I Can Be A Blessing To Today:

_____

Day 5: I Will Not Live In Fear

2 Timothy 1:7 For God has not given us a spirit of fear, but of power and of love and of a sound mind.

Father, thank You! Thank You for believing in me, even when it is hard for me to believe in myself. I pray that You would help me to abandon my old ways of thinking; the ones that hold me back from completely surrendering to Your will and purpose for my life. I ask for forgiveness for every time I let fear operate over faith. I ask for strength to be able to stand up and be strong, knowing that even though I may feel fear, I do not have to bow to it. I bow only to You. Everything must bow to You, even fear.

I lay my life in Your hands. I place my future, my plans, my thoughts, about what should be and what could be, in Your control. My desire is to honor and please You, so whatever that looks like or wherever that may take me, that is what I choose.

Fill me daily with Your power and love. When I go out in public I want to be dripping with the presence of God. I want people to feel Your love everywhere I go. I want people to feel hope when I walk in the room, not because I am there, but because of Your Spirit inside me. Help me be reminded daily, moment by moment that You are always with me and that I am never alone. I have no reason to be anxious when I have the maker of the oceans and the mountains living in me. I have nothing to fear. Fear is only a lie to make me believe that You are unable to do what You said You would do in my life.

Help me to cast down every vain imagination that tries to exalt itself above the knowledge of You. Nothing will be exalted higher in my life than Your Name and Your Will. Help me to draw closer to You daily. I love you. In Jesus Name I pray, amen.

Thought For The Day: Being courageous doesn't meant I won't ever feel fear, it means I will keep going, even when I feel it. I'm not lead by my feelings, I am lead by the Spirit of God.

Day 5

Notes (Go ahead and mark it up! The key is to be REAL. This is just you and God.)

_____

_____

_____

_____

_____

_____

_____

_____

_____

_____

5 Things I Am Thankful For Today Are:

_____

_____

_____

_____

_____

Today I Will Fast _____ for 8 hours.

Someone I Can Be A Blessing To Today:

_____

Day 6: I Am Your Treasure

Matthew 13:44-45 Again, the kingdom of heaven is like treasure hidden in a field, which a man found and hid; and for joy over it he goes and sells all that he has and buys that field. Again, the kingdom of heaven is like a merchant seeking beautiful pearls, who, when he had found one pearl of great price, went and sold all that he had and bought it.

Father, your kingdom, and the love and peace I have found in You are worth more than anything I could ever find in this world. I thank You for coming to rescue me before I even knew I needed to be saved. I am thankful that when You looked at the earth like the man in the parable looking at the field, You sold all You had to get me. You gave everything, even Your own life. To say thank You, I offer mine back to You. I offer all I am, all I have, all my dreams and plans. I put aside all the things I thought I wanted, I sell out to You. I belong to You. Where You lead me I will follow.

Teach me Your ways, oh God! Help me not to follow what this flesh wants to do, but to bring it into line with what Your Word says. I offer my body as a living sacrifice. My going to work, my grocery shopping, my house chores, my everyday living - I place it before You. I want to do every task to bring glory to Your Name. I want to live in excellence to honor You. I want to go the extra mile; to get my life in shape, just as a weight lifter does at the gym. Help me to work out my faith. Help me to buffet my body and use the Fruits of the Spirit You have put in me. Patience, self-control, love, joy, peace. Give me the strength to do the hard things and the bold moves You ask me to make.

Daily, I long to be closer to You. My soul cries to know You more; to know Your ways. Your Word refreshes my soul like cool water on a hot summer day. It breathes new life with every word I read. I don't know how people go through life not knowing You. I wouldn't want to get out of bed without first turning to You. Take me deeper. Bring me closer. Fill me with Your heart and help me to love everyone around me with the God kind of love, the kind that melts away bitterness and hurt, the healing kind of love. I love You. Thank You for loving me in such an amazing way. In Jesus Name I pray, amen.

Thought For The Day: I am not defined by this world. It does not determine my value. God alone determines that. To Him, I am worth it. I am loved. I am His.

Day 6

Notes (Go ahead and mark it up! The key is to be REAL. This is just you and God.)

_____

_____

_____

_____

_____

_____

_____

_____

_____

_____

5 Things I Am Thankful For Today Are:

_____

_____

_____

_____

_____

Today I Will Fast _____ for 8 hours.

Someone I Can Be A Blessing To Today:

_____

Day 7: Teach Me To Rest In You

Matthew 11:28-30 Come to Me, all *you* who labor and are heavy laden, and I will give you rest. Take My yoke upon you and learn from Me, for I am gentle and lowly in heart, and you will find rest for your souls. For My yoke *is* easy and My burden is light."

Father, I come to You today seeking Your will. I want to learn Your ways and find out the depths of Your heart; to find out what it means to be truly in close relationship with You.

Teach me to rest in You. Not to just set one day aside a week to not do any work, but to make every day the sabbath and rest in You. To be able to have rest in the deepest part of my soul, even when I may be going through stormy waters. I want to know what it means to face adversity without it rocking the inward makings of my soul. To have trouble on the outside, but Your peace that keeps me calm and steady on the inside.

I pray that You would help me soak up Your wisdom daily. To know what it means to truly walk with You, to have open, honest communication with You. Help me to bring everything to You first; You're the only one who can do anything about my situations anyway. Help me to simply pray about it and believe You are working. I have never seen you fail. You have always shown up right now time. You have never left me in disappointment. You have never left me stranded or abandoned. Your Word says You are a Friend who sticks closer than a brother. Help me to fully understand that.

My life is always more peaceful when I am trusting You. Help me to daily, moment by moment, put my trust in You - no matter what I may be facing, no matter what doctors report I may get, no matter who left my life, and no matter what situations may come my way. Help me to rest in Your love. I believe, through You, I can do big things in this life to bring honor and glory to Your Name. I have read exciting stories in The Bible and my prayer is that You will use me for something extraordinary. Through You, all things are possible and I receive Your will for my life. In the Name of Jesus I pray, amen.

Thought For The Day: Today, I will walk in peace, knowing that God is working in my situation. He promises to work all things to my good. I will rest in that.

Day 7

Notes (Go ahead and mark it up! The key is to be REAL. This is just you and God.)

_____

_____

_____

_____

_____

_____

_____

_____

_____

_____

5 Things I Am Thankful For Today Are:

_____

_____

_____

_____

_____

Today I Will Fast _____ for 8 hours.

Someone I Can Be A Blessing To Today:

_____

Day 8: I Will Take Up My Cross

Luke 9:23 Then He said to *them* all, "If anyone desires to come after Me, let him deny himself, and take up his cross daily, and follow Me."

Father, I come before You and bow my life before Your throne, giving You full access to every part of me. My heart, mind, body, soul, spirit, my strength, my will, my emotions, my time, my love and my finances are all in Your control.

I pray that You would empty me of selfishness and pride. I don't want anything getting in the way of my relationship with You. I will put no other gods before You. I will not put myself before You. I will lift Your statutes above my plans, for I am not my own.

Rid me of vain ambition or any foolish thing that may try to steal my attention from what really matters - You. Help me to walk in love knowing that love is not an emotion, but a choice I make every moment. Help me to love people the way You have loved me, so unconditionally, purely and without them having to earn it. Help me to offer love in every situation. Help me to shut my mouth and rid my life of gossip, for I know it is a poison that steals my joy. Help me to always give others the better seat; to give the advantage to others knowing I have my place and all I need is in You. Help me to be someone who sees the best in every person and calls it out in them with encouragement and an uplifting spirit.

Help me to love myself enough to say no to things I need to say no to. Help me to love myself in a way that causes me to be healthy in mind, body, soul, and spirit to better serve You. Help me take leaps of radical faith, the kind that remove me from my comfort zone and place me in an area where my trust is entirely in You. Help me to love myself in a way that I will not let people walk all over me. I have the King of the universe living in me, I am not a doormat, but I also do not walk all over others.

Help me to serve You with my best self, no matter what is going on in my life. I love you. In Jesus Name I pray, amen.

Thought For The Day: I will be a person who sees the very best in everyone and who speaks life over each of them. Every person has gold hidden in them, I will find it and call it forth so they can shine too.

Day 8

Notes (Go ahead and mark it up! The key is to be REAL. This is just you and God.)

_____

_____

_____

_____

_____

_____

_____

_____

_____

5 Things I Am Thankful For Today Are:

_____

_____

_____

_____

_____

Today I Will Fast _____ for 8 hours.

Someone I Can Be A Blessing To Today:

_____

Day 9: Help Me To Walk In Greater Love

1 John 3:16-18 By this we know love, because He laid down His life for us. And we also ought to lay down *our* lives for the brethren. But whoever has this world's goods, and sees his brother in need, and shuts up his heart from him, how does the love of God abide in him? My little children, let us not love in word or in tongue, but in deed and in truth.

Lord Jesus, help me to love like You love. I pray that every morning You would shower me in Your love, enough for me to spread around for the whole day to everyone I meet. I know it is Your love that changes people's hearts and gives hope. Help me to lay down what "I want," so Your love can shine through me. I pray that You would bless me to be a blessing, to be able to meet the needs of others so they can feel Your goodness and remember that You care for them.

Everything I have is Yours - You have full control. If You tell me to give something away, even if it is my favorite possession on this planet, I will do it knowing You always have a better plan than I do. Help me to give so freely and liberally, just as You do - not only of this world goods, but of mercy, love, grace and kindness, for those are the best things.

Your love is like a spring rainfall to the soul. It cleanses and refreshes as it washes completely over me. Help me to share that with others. For I have one goal on this earth: to help people find You and to come into a better relationship with You through Your love. For it is Your love that saved us from ourselves and from the enemy and changed my life forever.

I don't want to just talk about love with no action. I pray that You would guide me in ways to shine Your light everywhere I go and in everything I do. My life is not my own, You have full control.

Help me to know Your love more and to better understand how someone so Holy can love someone like me, someone who is so fragile and wavering. Help me to always remember that it is not by works I am saved or loved, but by salvation and grace alone. Where would I be had it not been for the hand of The Lord that was on my side? Lord, I love you with all my heart and everything I am. Today, help me to love You even more. In Jesus Name I pray, amen.

Thought For The Day: I will go out today and give out His love everywhere I go. My smile says it all - I am loved by The King. I will put the needs of others before myself and do everything I do unto Jesus.

Day 9

Notes (Go ahead and mark it up! The key is to be REAL. This is just you and God.)

5 Things I Am Thankful For Today Are:

_____

_____

_____

_____

_____

Today I Will Fast _____ for 8 hours.

Someone I Can Be A Blessing To Today:

_____

Day 10: God I Want More Of You

Mathew 6:16-18 Moreover, when you fast, do not be like the hypocrites, with a sad countenance. For they disfigure their faces that they may appear to men to be fasting. Assuredly, I say to you, they have their reward. But you, when you fast, anoint your head and wash your face, so that you do not appear to men to be fasting, but to your Father who *is* in the secret *place;* and your Father who sees in secret will reward you openly.

Father, I come seeking Your face and Your will. I know Mathew 6:16 says WHEN you fast, not if you fast... Help me to make fasting part of my life. Not just with meals, but in every area. I give You full access to prune what needs pruning. Help me to make radical choices for You in the secret place. Help me to fast with my time and with social media. With meals, television, and all other aspects of life. Help me to fast so I can get my life into balance, with You at the center of it all.

I don't want to play the role of a victim. I want to be a mighty warrior for Your kingdom. Help me to grow in the Spirit. I know it will not be comfortable and I will have to say no to some things and get rid of some things, but I place a high value on what You have in store for me. The stakes are too high for me to settle.

Help me to evaluate the people I have surrounded myself with. Give me discernment so that I will not be connected to people who might be a bad influence on my life or lead me down the wrong path. I know that not everyone who smiles at me is "for" me. I pray that You would send people into my life who will fight for and with me. Good Godly friends are valuable. Help me to be an encourager to those around me, to build people up and not tear them down. My words are so powerful, help me to use them to add to Your kingdom. Help me to deflect negative words from others so they don't make a home in me. I have no place for them.

Help me to live my life before an audience of One - You. Help me not to put so much emphasis on what people around me may think of me. I don't want pride and self image to get in the way of my relationship with You. I want to be fully surrendered. Help me to fast, and while I do, help me to know You more. Guide me in a better way to live. Teach me during my everyday living. Help me not to fast just for the sake of fasting, but to do it with passion knowing that You are the prize. You are what I am seeking after. You are everything.

Thought For The Day: I will keep laying myself down daily for Him. Anything I cannot let go of has a hold on me. I will not live in chains.

Day 10

Notes (Go ahead and mark it up! The key is to be REAL. This is just you and God.)

_____

_____

_____

_____

_____

_____

_____

_____

_____

_____

5 Things I Am Thankful For Today Are:

_____

_____

_____

_____

_____

Today I Will Fast _____ for 8 hours.

Someone I Can Be A Blessing To Today:

_____

Day 11: Keep Reminding Me Who I Am

James 1:22-24 But be doers of the word, and not hearers only, deceiving yourselves. For if anyone is a hearer of the word and not a doer, he is like a man observing his natural face in a mirror; for he observes himself, goes away, and immediately forgets what kind of man he was.

Father, I come to You with my heart bowed and my mind receptive, looking to honor You and gain wisdom from You. Help me to daily look into the mirror of Your Word so that I won't forget who I am. Help me to thirst for Your Word more each day. I pray You would give me a revelation of how You see me through Your Word. I know that apart from You, I am nothing. I know if I can get a glimpse of how You see me, it will change my whole world.

Your Word says I am strong, even when I feel that I am at my weakest. Your Word says I am blessed when I come and blessed when I go, blessed in the city and blessed in the country. You say I am the righteousness of Christ. I receive all of this right now in Jesus' name. I may not even fully comprehend what it all means yet, but Lord I am willing to learn - show me who I am in You.

I want to be able to 'do' the Word. Help me to hear, not just with my ears, but with my heart. Re-program me to think like You think. Help me to grow up and put away childish ways and mindsets. I want to know the fullness of You in my life. Write Your Words on my heart so that my automatic response in every situation is Your Word, not my thoughts.

Let no bitterness take root in me. Your Word says to forgive, just as Christ has forgiven us. Help me to do that. Help me to remember that this life is only a vapor and it is not worth holding onto things like that.

Fear and anxiety have no place in me. Your Word says to 'fear not' and that is what I will do. It is as simple as that. You wouldn't say it if You were not able to back it up. Help me to trust You, no matter what. Thank You for guiding me each day into a closer relationship with You. My life will be spent giving You honor and praise for all You have done. In the most powerful Name in Heaven and earth I pray, in Jesus Name, amen.

Thought For The Day: Reading my Bible is not window shopping, thinking "one day I'll be like that.." It's discovering what God has placed down in me and who I already am in Him.

Day 11

Notes (Go ahead and mark it up! The key is to be REAL. This is just you and God.)

_____

_____

_____

_____

_____

_____

_____

_____

_____

_____

5 Things I Am Thankful For Today Are:

_____

_____

_____

_____

_____

Today I Will Fast _____ for 8 hours.

Someone I Can Be A Blessing To Today:

_____

Day 12: I Keep Pressing On

Philippians 3:13-14 Brethren, I do not count myself to have apprehended; but one thing *I do*, forgetting those things which are behind and reaching forward to those things which are ahead, I press toward the goal for the prize of the upward call of God in Christ Jesus.

God, today I lay out before You a heart that had to do some pressing. I have pressed through days I thought I would never make it through. You have always been there. I pray You would help me continue to press. Help me to move further into the Spirit, deeper and deeper. I need more of Your glory, more of Your presence in my life. I need the Holy Spirit dwelling in my every thought like a sweet, gentle breeze, guiding me in the ways I should go.

Help me to forget those things that are behind me. A lot of it wasn't fair. A lot of it, I even brought on myself. Some of the things I went through still don't make sense, but I'm choosing to trust You anyway. Your word promises that all things are working together for my good and I believe that. Help me to throw off anything I have been carrying around that has been weighing me down. It is so easy to look over my past and have shame and regret for the things I have said and done, but moment by moment, You continue to heal me and wash away the residue of my past. You've let it go, help me to let it go too. I toss my entire past, every mistake, and every sin into the sea of Your forgiveness, never to hold it against myself again.

I know my best days are still out in front of me and I reach forth and press on to what You have for me. I don't want to just stay in one spot, I want to break camp and keep moving towards You. I need to move on from some of these things, to stop carrying them around. I pray that You would continue to help me heal, daily, bringing restoration and wholeness in every area, while strengthening me through the process. Make me a bold warrior for Christ. In the name of Jesus I pray, Amen.

Thought For The Day: Today, I can make a list of action items to help me move in the direction He has called me. I may not arrive today, but I can start moving right now. I am strong enough. I have what it takes. I will keep pressing.

Day 12

Notes (Go ahead and mark it up! The key is to be REAL. This is just you and God.)

_____

_____

_____

_____

_____

_____

_____

_____

_____

_____

5 Things I Am Thankful For Today Are:

_____

_____

_____

_____

_____

Today I Will Fast _____ for 8 hours.

Someone I Can Be A Blessing To Today:

_____

Day 13: Today, I Choose You Again

Psalm 65:4 Blessed *is the man* You choose, And cause to approach *You, That* he may dwell in Your courts. We shall be satisfied with the goodness of Your house, Of Your holy temple.

Father, Thank You that You chose us, long before we chose You. Thank You for inviting me into Your holy place to draw my heart closer to You. Help me to lay anything down that may be holding me from coming in closer. Renew my mind and set me free from any wrong thinking. Wash over me with a song of Your love as I know that is what cleanses the eyes of my soul to be able to see things like You see them.

Fill me with a hunger for Your Spirit. Set a fire in my soul that is not easily quenched. Burn in me with a light that shines so bright of Your glory, so I can be a city on a hill pointing others in the direction to find You.

You are the only thing in my life that remains steady. Your love for me never changes as human love does. Your love for me is not based on what I do, but on who You are. Remind me who I am in You continually, letting Your ways be ever-present in my thoughts and in my heart.

I am blessed that You chose me, that You would even look my way. I pray that You would keep me close to You, that I will forever dwell right beside You in close communion with You. Don't let me stray. This world is full of things that continually try to pull me away. There are things that pull on me daily to steal my attention, but I will keep my eyes on You. I choose You, over and over and over. I choose you.

Thought For The Day: Everyday, I am faced with a battle for my attention, but by choice, my eyes remain on Him.

Day 13

Notes (Go ahead and mark it up! The key is to be REAL. This is just you and God.)

_____

_____

_____

_____

_____

_____

_____

_____

_____

_____

5 Things I Am Thankful For Today Are:

_____

_____

_____

_____

_____

Today I Will Fast _____ for 8 hours.

Someone I Can Be A Blessing To Today:

_____

Day 14: I Ask For Wisdom God

Colossians 3:16-17 Let the word of Christ dwell in you richly in all wisdom, teaching and admonishing one another in psalms and hymns and spiritual songs, singing with grace in your hearts to the Lord. And whatever you do in word or deed, *do* all in the name of the Lord Jesus, giving thanks to God the Father through Him.

Father. I bow my heart, my mind, my emotions, all that I am and all that I have, to You right now. I give You control. You are the first and the last. You are beginning and the end. You know all things. Search my heart God. Help me to walk closer to You each day.

I devote my works to You. I know I am not saved by works, but the work I do, my job, my everyday living, I devote it to You. Help me to honor You with every step I take and every word I say. Help me to keep Your love in my heart and on my lips, singing Your praises through everything. When I feel like it and when I don't, because I am not driven by what I feel, I live by what I know. I know You are good.

Help me to walk in excellence. Let everything I do be a sweet smell that rises up as I live my life as an offering unto You.

I pray for wisdom - The God kind of wisdom which only comes from above. The things You teach me are not found in books, they are only found in Your presence. I pray You would give me inventions and innovations. I pray that You would show me things in the Spirit which would cause me to manifest Your greatness in the earth. I pray You would cover me in Your glory and let Your presence be all around me.

I pray that You would show me the way - Your divine way. You always have the best plan. In my own strength I am nothing, but with You, I know I am more than enough.

Father, whisper Your love into my heart and let it flow into the deepest depths of my soul. Let it wash over me in the most beautiful way, bringing cleansing and peace to my inner spirit.

Help me to lay down what I think I know and always be ready to grow, to come up higher. Help me to always be willing to admit when I am wrong or when I have outgrown old ways of thinking. I want to live for You in the best way possible to live a life that is full of Your power, love, and mercy.

Help me to give out the wisdom You give to me so others can live better too. Help me to remember that the more people I share Your love and light with, the better place this world will be.

Thought For The Day: A hug can change someones life, especially if they are in the middle of a storm.

Day 14

Notes (Go ahead and mark it up! The key is to be REAL. This is just you and God.)

_____

_____

_____

_____

_____

_____

_____

_____

_____

_____

5 Things I Am Thankful For Today Are:

_____

_____

_____

_____

_____

Today I Will Fast _____ for 8 hours.

Someone I Can Be A Blessing To Today:

_____

Day 15: Wake Us Up, God!

Romans 13:11-14 And *do* this, knowing the time, that now *it is* high time to awake out of sleep; for now our salvation *is* nearer than when we *first* believed. The night is far spent, the day is at hand. Therefore let us cast off the works of darkness, and let us put on the armor of light. Let us walk properly, as in the day, not in revelry and drunkenness, not in lewdness and lust, not in strife and envy. But put on the Lord Jesus Christ, and make no provision for the flesh, to *fulfill its* lusts.

Father, Thank You for your love. I know it is the power that breaks every chain. It brings healing and restoration in every area. It also brings correction and keeps me in line. Just like the verse says, it is high time to awake out of this deep sleep. Help me to keep focus in this hour, to put away the works of the flesh. Guide me in letting go of all unforgiveness and letting go of bitterness and strife. Temptations come daily, but You have made a way for me to escape them all through the power and strength of Your love.

I know these things. I know the weight of carrying around guilt and shame are too heavy. I know that forgiving quickly so that it doesn't have time to settle into my soul is very important. I know that to satisfy the lust of the flesh in a moment of hastiness is never worth the price paid in the long run. I know all these things in my mind, help me to know them in my actions, in my comings and goings. Help me to be so fast to do whatever Your Word says. It is final authority in my life. I choose it over my own ways. I pray for a deeper connection with your Spirit to guide me in all truth, all day long. I need you God, I cant do this alone. Never in all my trying will I get it right, only when I rest in Your grace I realize You have made me righteous and I am living from a place of Holiness, not striving for it as an unattainable prize.

Help me have clarity in every situation. In these last days, I don't want to waste a single day. Help me to value what you value and honor what you honor. With every temptation, help me to call on Your Name. Help me to run away from sin so fast the devil's head spins. Lord, help me to keep my eyes on the only thing I have found that has ever really mattered - You. I recommit myself to you today and everyday, I am only Yours. In the name of Jesus I pray, amen.

Thought For The Day: I am in charge of how I act. I can make the necessary changes in my life to be who I am called to be. I have the power. I can do this.

Day 15

Notes (Go ahead and mark it up! The key is to be REAL. This is just you and God.)

_____

_____

_____

_____

_____

_____

_____

_____

_____

5 Things I Am Thankful For Today Are:

_____

_____

_____

_____

_____

Today I Will Fast _____ for 8 hours.

Someone I Can Be A Blessing To Today:

_____

Day 16: Prayer From The Heart

This prayer devotional is meant to be a guide to help in your personal prayer time and bible study. Today, pick a verse from the bible. Maybe it is one of your favorite verses or one you have read recently. Go back and read a few verses before and after the verse you are thinking of. This will help you put it into context and get the full picture of what is being said.

For todays prayer, I want you to pray your own words. Pray about whatever you are going through today. Be real, open, and honest. The most important thing you can do is be willing and ready to say yes to whatever you hear the spirit speaks to you about. Prayer is nothing more than communication with God. You don't have to use fancy words or know all of the scriptures by heart, God hears you.

I like to go into a room where I know there will not be many distractions for a while, somewhere I can physically get down and bow myself before Him. *(Use the lines below to write some things you prayed about so you can come back to them later.)*

If you don't know where to start, start by saying this:
Father, I bow down to you right now and give You all I have…
Write it down, or even just the main parts of it, on the next page.

Day 16

_____

_____

_____

_____

_____

_____

_____

_____

Thought For The Day: Whether I am on a mountain, in a valley, or somewhere far in between, I can call out to God. Geography can't hide Him. He is as close as my next breathe.

Day 16

Notes (Go ahead and mark it up! The key is to be REAL. This is just you and God.)

_____

_____

_____

_____

_____

_____

_____

_____

_____

_____

5 Things I Am Thankful For Today Are:

_____

_____

_____

_____

_____

Today I Will Fast _____ for 8 hours.

Someone I Can Be A Blessing To Today:

_____

Day 17: Lord, Change My Perspective

1 Peter 2:1-3 Therefore, laying aside all malice, all deceit, hypocrisy, envy, and all evil speaking, as newborn babes, desire the pure milk of the word, that you may grow thereby, if indeed you have tasted that the Lord *is* gracious.

God, I pray that You would empty me of all self-worship and self-glorification. I give You an all-access pass to make any changes that are needed. My heart longs for You. I lay everything down at Your throne, any part of me that has a "me first" spirit. I lay down my mind, will and emotions and choose this day to follow You, no matter where you lead. Flow in me like streams of clean, fresh mountain water. Purify me. Wash over me again and again.

Guide me in radical obedience to Your word. Help me to believe Your word over any other opinion, including my own. My pridefulness sometimes tells me that my ways are better or that I can find a faster way than waiting upon You. I get myself in trouble sometimes when I am too impatient to wait on You. Yet, again and again Your grace shows up like the sun shining on a early spring morning, steadfast and always right on time. Help me to know You, to know what it means to be known by You. God help me to give myself to you fully and completely, in every season, in every moment.

More of you Lord! Less of what I think and want. God, You are the prize. We spend so much time and energy chasing things in this world, but when it comes down to it, none of these things matter. Everything we see around us will eventually end up in a junk pile somewhere and I don't want to waste my life on things that are here today and gone tomorrow. I set my sights on things eternal. Help me to rise up and take the high road, the narrow path. Help me to live that way in every decision. Help me to see everyone I meet as a soul who needs to be restored by Christ, to see them as person who, just like me, wanted to be accepted and loved. Help me to share that love and most of all, Your overwhelming, life-changing Gospel.

Thought For The Day: Every person I meet will someday go to Heaven or Hell. I could be the one who shares the good news with them. I could be the reason someone's life gets changed forever.

Day 17

Notes (Go ahead and mark it up! The key is to be REAL. This is just you and God.)

_____

_____

_____

_____

_____

_____

_____

_____

_____

_____

5 Things I Am Thankful For Today Are:

_____

_____

_____

_____

_____

Today I Will Fast _____ for 8 hours.

Someone I Can Be A Blessing To Today:

_____

Day 18: Lord, Lead Us Into Unity

Colossians 3:13-15 Bearing with one another, and forgiving one another, if anyone has a complaint against another; even as Christ forgave you, so you also *must do*. 14 But above all these things put on love, which is the bond of perfection. 15 And let the peace of God rule in your hearts, to which also you were called in one body; and be thankful.

God, I pray for unity in the body of Christ. Without it, we are powerless, but we need You to help make it happen. Please forgive me for every time I have caused discord among the saints of God and in the church community. This flesh gets the best of me sometimes, but I don't want to make excuses. Help me to do better, to rise higher and to always choose to treat others in a way that builds unity for the kingdom of God. Please help me to avoid petty drama and disagreements, no matter what I have to do.

God, I need healing in my heart and mind. I need You to patch up all the broken spots and bring wholeness to every area inside my soul that has lack. Make up for anything I have missed out on in life. Become my fullness. Be the reason I can take a deep breathe and smile again. Sometimes the storms rage inside me, and I have to admit that sometimes I don't even know why. My flesh wars against itself and I'm caught in the middle. These things are many of the reasons I have settled for less along the way. These things are the reason I haven't lived in unity. I pray You would break the cycle that keeps me from striving for unity. Help me make it a priority to seek out other Christians in my region and connect with them. We can all agree on one thing: Jesus. Open doors for me to bring unity to my region in a way that has never been seen before! Move in my city in a way that even the news media comes to do a story. Move in a way that changes our culture. Come and have your way in our hearts, Lord. In the name of Jesus I pray, amen.

Thought For The Day: Maybe I'm the Hand, maybe I'm the Foot, but whatever my part in the body of Christ, I will not compare it to what someone else is called to do. God formed me and planned me, I'm right where I'm supposed to be.

Day 18

Notes (Go ahead and mark it up! The key is to be REAL. This is just you and God.)

---

5 Things I Am Thankful For Today Are:

_____

_____

_____

_____

_____

Today I Will Fast _____ for 8 hours.

Someone I Can Be A Blessing To Today:

_____

Day 19: A Prayer For My Region

1 Timothy 2:1-2 Therefore I exhort first of all that supplications, prayers, intercessions, *and* giving of thanks be made for all men, for kings and all who are in authority, that we may lead a quiet and peaceable life in all godliness and reverence.

Father, I come before You to lay myself down and lift my leaders up. I pray for the president of this great nation, regardless of my political preferences. I pray You would protect the president and provide wisdom for leadership. We need a robust and Godly commander-in-chief who will listen to You.

I pray for our local leaders, our city council, and other decision-making authorities that they would open their hearts and ears to You and Your ways. I pray for revival in the courts! I pray for revival in our government. I pray Your Spirit would be poured out on all flesh! Renew us and refresh us with Your Spirit!

I pray for the local pastors in this region and the burden they bear to bring forth Your Word. I pray a hedge of protection around them and that You would strengthen them as they fight the good fight of faith. I pray for our region, that it would be set on fire with the fire of the Holy Spirit and that You do the work that only You can do. We need You to show up and take over. Our ways don't work God, help us to stop messing things up with the works of the flesh.

We need You to make every crooked place straight. Be a light unto our path. We need You to send revival fire from heaven. USE ME, LORD! Use me to spread Your fire and the knowledge of Your great love. Equip our local leaders with boldness to minister to people who have been cast aside by the church. Help us to reach these people and help them be restored through Your precious blood!

Let Your healing and love come in like a flood. We desperately need Your touch Lord. Our land needs healing. Our hearts cry is to see You move. Embrace us with a fresh wind from Heaven that changes the hearts of the people. We need real and lasting change. We need reform that is rooted and grounded in Your never-ending, life-changing love.

Thought For The Day: I may be just one person, but with the power of God, I can make way for His presence to bring about a revival that can touch the nations!

Day 19

Notes (Go ahead and mark it up! The key is to be REAL. This is just you and God.)

_____

_____

_____

_____

_____

_____

_____

_____

_____

5 Things I Am Thankful For Today Are:

_____

_____

_____

_____

_____

Today I Will Fast _____ for 8 hours.

Someone I Can Be A Blessing To Today:

_____

Day 20: Prayer For My Enemies

Matthew 5:43-45 You have heard that it was said, 'You shall love your neighbor and hate your enemy.' But I say to you, love your enemies, bless those who curse you, do good to those who hate you, and pray for those who spitefully use you and persecute you, that you may be sons of your Father in heaven; for He makes His sun rise on the evil and on the good, and sends rain on the just and on the unjust.

Father, I need Your help! I have all these mixed emotions trying to lead me off path. I know what Your Word says about forgiving and praying for my enemies. I know I must forgive, even if it wasn't fair... Even if the other person is not sorry for what they have done. I know I need to move on from this and I need You to help me do it with a clean heart.

Do a deep work in me Father. I cannot lay this down on my own, please help me. The thoughts I still have towards these situations seem to get the best of me. I choose right now to honor You and Your way above how I feel. I choose right now in the Name of Jesus to forgive. I CHOOSE. The rest of me may take a while to catch up. My feelings may take a minute to get the memo that I have chosen to lay this down completely. The Bible says that You are my vindicator, so I am trusting You to work all of this our for my good.

I don't want to wish bad things on other people. Help me to pray blessings over those who have done me wrong. Help me to send gifts to and bless the people who have lied about me. I know I never have to accept these people back into my "close circle of friends," but I want any desire within me that wants to see them fail, or that wishes something bad on another person to go away, right now in Jesus' Name. Lord, please forgive me for carrying around bitterness and resentment. Forgive me for all the time I wasted being mad in a situation I couldn't have done much about. Help me to truly move on. I ask it with a sincere heart, in the Name of Jesus. Show me how to Love, Lord. Amen.

Thought For The Day: It has been said that unforgiveness is like drinking poison hoping the other person gets sick. I have been forgiven much, I will forgive my fellow man the same.

Day 20

Notes (Go ahead and mark it up! The key is to be REAL. This is just you and God.)

_____

_____

_____

_____

_____

_____

_____

_____

_____

_____

5 Things I Am Thankful For Today Are:

_____

_____

_____

_____

_____

Today I Will Fast _____ for 8 hours.

Someone I Can Be A Blessing To Today:

_____

Day 21: Honor

2 Corinthians 5:16-19 Therefore, from now on, we regard no one according to the flesh. Even though we have known Christ according to the flesh, yet now we know Him thus no longer. Therefore, if anyone is in Christ, he is a new creation; old things have passed away; behold, all things have become new. Now all things are of God, who has reconciled us to Himself through Jesus Christ, and has given us the ministry of reconciliation.

Father, thank You for saving my soul! I was in deep trouble when You came and rescued me. Frankly, I don't know what my life would be like if You hadn't shown up when You did. It was right on time and I can't thank You enough!

I want to share that life changing moment with someone else. I want others to be able to experience what I have experienced. I pray that You would use me in a mighty way to see the lives of others transformed, the way You changed mine.

Help me to regard every soul as precious and valuable. Help me to have a passion and a zeal lit deep in me that burns for the spreading of Your Word! Help me to shine bright as a beacon of hope, not for my own glory or boasting, but as a light that shines toward the cross and lights it up for the world to see You.

Use me God to spread Your word! Use me in this hour to be one who forgets my own interests and to set my sights on the things above! Help me to escape the traps set by this world to get entangled in the business of life and forget what you have called me to. I know I am here for such a time as this! Keep me wide awake and of sober mind during these times so that I may finish my race strong as you have called me to do.

Help me to show honor to every individual. You personally came and shed Your blood for each and every one of us. Help me to see each person with that same value. The valuable blood of Jesus. Help me to honor and hold in high regard each person as they are precious in Your sight. Help me to also see them as precious in my sight. It all comes down to Your love. Let it grow in me like a mighty fruit bearing seed, bringing life, abundance and your goodness everywhere I go. I want to value what You value above all else. In the name of Jesus I pray, Amen.

Thought For The Day: Life is short. While I'm here, I plan on making it count. I will live boldly today!

Day 21

Notes (Go ahead and mark it up! The key is to be REAL. This is just you and God.)

_____

_____

_____

_____

_____

_____

_____

_____

_____

_____

5 Things I Am Thankful For Today Are:

_____

_____

_____

_____

_____

Today I Will Fast _____ for 8 hours.

Someone I Can Be A Blessing To Today:

_____

About The Author

Josh Paul is an author, evangelist, recording artist, television show host, and founder of Anchor Ridge. His life's mission is to see more than 100,000,000 people come to Christ before he leaves earth. He utilizes the airwaves, music, books and live events to encourage, uplift and help people by introducing them to Christ.

Josh can be found on many of your favorite television networks, on his popular show "Anchor Today with Josh Paul" or being interviewed on other widely recognized Christian television shows.

"If I can make someone's life better, that is what I want to do. Whether it is building a house for a family who doesn't have one, giving groceries to the poor, sharing Christ with a successful businessman, or visiting a lonely widow or the elderly at a nursing home. It all comes down to Christ. He is the only thing of value we have that we can give someone. We can dole out all we have to everyone we meet, but if we do not give them Christ, we have given them nothing of true value. I hope this book emboldens people to share Christ with everyone they know."

-Josh Paul

No one can do it for you.

You must

choose

to

go

out

and

make

every

single

day

the

very
best.

God is with you.